Women

in

PURSUIT

of

Happiness

ELANDRA FOGLE

Table of Contents

.

Introduction

The book *In Pursuit of Happiness* is a guide to helping women discover their value, worth, and happiness. Happiness is a gift, the ultimate fulfillment of our hearts. It is an essential need that every human being looks to achieve. As you read each page of this manual, you will find out how to establish healthy relationships. Readers will come to understand that *happiness* is not defined by the materialistic things possessed in life, but a fundamental key to obtaining success in the philosophy of life. God needed me to remind every woman that she is a Queen and special in His sight. Yes, women were created for so much more. I hope every reader will gain strength in finding her purpose and be encouraged. Within the trenches of these pages, each woman will learn how to respect, care, and love herself.

My prayer is that every person will find the ultimate fulfillment and satisfaction with their life's aspirations. I hope that this book will be a roadmap to finding that special someone who can truly bring a lifetime of happiness.

May all your dreams become a thousand stars, so hold on tight.

1

In Pursuit of Happiness

For many centuries women find men to be the object of our affection, the center of our attraction, and the focus of our attention. We tend to love everything about men, whether it's good or bad, and sometimes it doesn't make any difference in our eyes. Many women still have this sense of desire to be loved by our opposite, the male component. One of the prime motives that drive some women to chase after a man is because we are always in pursuit of happiness. There is such a need in a woman who lacks affection or when she has very little self-control over her emotions. Many women may not feel this way, but others do.

Whereas, when a woman is striving to find that perfect man, she looks for the one who compliments her taste and keeps her happy. So much so that a woman who is desperate for love will do anything to obtain that level of satisfaction. We don't mind leaving behind relationships with our family and friends or letting go of a girlfriend who was a true friend just to obtain what we want.

Let me establish an understanding that, by nature, women are very emotional beings; it's a natural-born trait of ours, one of the instinctive explanations for why we love men the way that we do. Love itself is a basic element that all human beings need. However, when love is precipitated and given properly, we as women do expect it back, in hopes that men will love us the way we love them. However, under certain circumstances, in certain relationships, love is not always equally dispensed among the halves of the couple. This also depends on where both parties stand. Now I think men are strong beings, especially in their masculinity. They are beautiful, irresistible beings who we come across daily. I do admit that men are adorable and conventional with wisdom, and I'm speaking from a woman's perspective. I believe that men are the prized possessions to different women, at least in their own eyes. That's why we will fight tooth and nail for a man, giving so much of ourselves in exchange for what little affection they give, because we deserve it. When it comes to both genders, men are thinkers while women are talkers, which is a distinction between the genders as to how each party functions from an emotional level. Men may be good at communicating and expressing some of their thoughts, but not all at once because they don't always articulate their feelings the way we expect them to. These are just some of the characteristic traits of how men are made to function and operate concerning interaction in relationships.

On the other hand, women are talkers. A woman utilize communication as a way to express her personal feelings, emotions, and interest toward the man of her choice. However, when bringing the two together from a relational point of view, both genders play a role in contributing necessities to each other's lives. It is some woman's dream to find that perfect man that we propose will fulfill us. What we imagine as the ultimate goal to our happiness, which can be determined by a course of our own actions, contributes to the stimulation of imagination for a successful relationship.

We can distinguish the value of true love when it presents itself. Real love should never be defined through the material possessions that people use to determine their value for each other. Many find love based on obtaining resources such as money, cars, houses, fame, fortune, sex, men, and use all kinds of malicious acts to prove this is what love is all about. There are many other entities that are actually irrelevant to the main focus and revolve around love. Love was never intended to be identified by earthly possessions used to keep one satisfied. I believe that it goes much deeper and beyond the surface of any natural elements in existence, which surround the outside physical environment that is common to man. As human beings, we can compartmentalize our emotional dilemmas on a wide spectrum of relationships in so many areas that cater to our needs.

3

First, we must understand the association between the physiology and chemistry that is connected to our physical and sexual nature. We internalize our emotional state for companionship in terms of knowing the purpose for male/female compatibility to each other.

When making a comparison in accommodating both party's needs, we can use an object that is relevant to the importance for relationships. A magnet is a powerful force that attracts certain objects to itself and repels others. This is how chemistry works in our nature. It sends signals to our inner emotional beings to create those physical attractions to the opposite gender. Now we see what is the cause and effect that births these different emotions and feelings that develop from inside us.

Relationships are vital to our existence, because they play a role in every dimension of our lives. Relationships are necessary for how we communicate our thoughts, ideas, opinions, views, and many other aspects of our lives that revolve around this matter. Relationships are like a laboratory in search of a cure for an incurable disease. The researchers are constantly experimenting with different formulas, searching for a reaction to see what works and will cure the disease. If any success is found, then the answer to the problem has been found. With that said, this is how we explore relationships upon looking to establish companionship with the person who is our complement in different areas.

Qualities Men Possess

There are certain qualities in men that women are just crazy about. They're not just based on the tall, dark, and handsome guy, because we have the choice of admiring men from all walks of life. There are certain qualities about men that make a woman go weak in the knees, especially if she is already head over heels in love with how he makes her feel. She loses her marbles at times being in his arms because he's the man of her dreams. Now, while you might be thinking it's all about the finesse, I'd rather you think again because it goes a little deeper than the physical features of a person. There's more to men than meets the eye. Attraction is based on the potential mixture of physical attributes and, of course, that important emotional touch that women need. Each woman has certain things she looks for in a man, and how he presents himself can be a signal of what he brings to the table.

Basic Men's Qualities

For example, some women like men who are well groomed versus one who is a little sloppy. However, what her taste is will determine if this is the ideal candidate she's looking for in a relationship. It's not necessarily that tall is the important thing, but the reality is that height is not as important a part of how you present yourself. Just as men like a woman who keeps herself maintained, women, too, take interest in men who ensure that they are perfectly groomed or that *GQ*-type they're looking for. The basic thing most women believe is that if he is careful enough to take care of himself, then he can be trusted to take care of her. Remember, fellows, your appearance is the first impression you make on a woman that will hold her attention. Maybe it could land you that first date you're hoping for. On the other hand, maybe not all women are looking for the well-groomed type of man. Some women don't mind a sloppily dressed man; the guy who never combed his hair just might be a natural thing for him. Or he may not be a guy who takes out the time to swing by a shop to get a quick manicure. He doesn't mind wearing those wrinkled shirts or baggie jeans she likes. Men can come off as male chauvinists who do not care about making an impression on someone from the opposite sex, especially if they're only out for sex.

Her Taste

Women would rather a man give, and shower her with expensive gifts. Or even if she's a spoiled brat who is used to getting her way through seduction or exchange of monetary gifts. It's really a game called risky business, because by all means she knows what she wants and how to make her demands, even at the risk of being naughty but played at the same time. She's willing to take a chance at his offer because in that she finds comfort and love as a way to escape the emptiness she feels.

The Humorous Moments

Women for the most part possess a sense of humor. Having so much baggage of our own that we carry is more than enough burden to deal with, and we don't really care to entertain the company of another equally depressed soul. Yes, we are hit in the face with bad days, but it goes a long way if you have a zesty sense of humor, and clean humor at that. Beware, taking a crack at another women by constantly putting her down doesn't necessarily give you a upper hand either. However, different women like a man with a sense of humor. Not too serious at all times, but can crack a joke or two sometimes.

Emotional Care

Some women need constant reassurance that they are loved and cared for. The acts of intimacy can be shown in various ways, such as holding hands while strolling around the mall, watching a movie, or an occasional hug and kiss on the cheek following a hot date out and making sure she gets home safely. It is grand when a man can appreciate her at all times; at the same time, this is what pleases her and makes her smile.

The million-dollar smile

There's a reason women absolutely adore men with that million-dollar smile, and it has everything to do with pearly white teeth or the stars that glitter in the eyes. Believe it when she says that lights up her world, making her feel very special like there is no other man in her universe.

Calmness

Woman are known to be calm, cool, and collected. Now, I must admit they get hyped up quite easily, and that is the precise reason why the opposite component needs to be the calming factor in their lives. It really makes a difference if you don't stress out or fly off the handle at any and every incident. Your sex appeal lies as much in your personality as it does in your attitude: Women like men with a cool and peaceful attitude, someone who can calm them down and reassure them that all is well.

2

Competitors in the Marketplace

What are the chances for a woman securing e good man she has had her eyes on for quite some time among the countless other faces who are after the same thing she's looking to score? The odds can be low when the competition is on the table. Yes, this means war. This creates a battleground for contention and strife because of what they will do for love when the focus continues to be about men. Competition can be at its highest peak when competing for the love of a man. They have an old saying: you're not the only chip on the block.

It is in our nature to be competitive at every level of society. This falls on a wide category of things, such as education, business, careers, cars, houses, money, fashion, hair, clothes, beauty, and other material possession used to measure success. This example is why women are ready to attack for love, because they feel threatened by opponents at losing the chance to get firsthand access. Let's evaluate how women think on the basis of winning a competition. Every woman is born with a gift of intuition to recognize when something is wrong. With that said, when another woman is after the same man she likes, she can sense their motive also. Only then, when feelings of insecurity kick in, does competition become her best friend. Women continue to fight over nothing more than they fight over men. Her mechanism is a wall of defense, for all guards are up, her ego is on the rise, and her options become few. Some compete to land a dude, to look beautiful, or to fight for a man's attention because they feel he is the good guy. That's grand and this might be her opportunity to secure him. Along with these attributes comes an attitude behind certain behaviors, which can lead to a power struggle for love. Women will never give up on things they want badly, even at the risk of a man who is off limits. They become possessive, play tricks, and act stubborn just to see if they can get what they want. So here is the game of manipulation of trying to win him with her dressing, flirtatious walk, talk, and romance. If there are any feelings of insecurity, jealousy, or threat, she will work diligently by any means necessary to be in the spotlight. Intimidation can occur at any given time; if so, this will escalate the competition far more than what was initially expected. As tension builds up more, so does the desire because they are determined and confident they are coming out the winner. Some women can be selfish, self-centered, arrogant, insensitive, and non-caring toward their competitors. They think of themselves as a more suitable mate than the other candidates. We are very confrontational over men and have always been. The fighting comes as no surprise when eliminating another woman's chance to mingle and get close to the man they love, and the competition will go on until the man reveals his decision.

My friend Mel shared her traumatic experience of how cruel other women were to her, making her feel they were much better than she was. I'm sure many of us can identify with her pain. She experienced in her teens how women can be so insecure that they resort to putting another woman down. She was always a small and petite girl. As she grew older, she remains that size. It ran in her gene pool. She remembers an incident when she was seventeen and attracted the attention of a man she had a secret crush on but she was too shy or insecure about herself to approach him. He was also being pursued by other women. It so happens that most of the girls who liked this guy were curvier than Mel was. But she found out later that he was more attracted to petite women. These girls went out of their way to insult her, calling her anorexic, and telling her a real man wants some meat on their bones, and so on. Their words really affected her and how she felt about herself. She always wanted to be a bit bigger, and admired the curvaceous women. After a while, she became very insecure about herself and remained in a shell for half of her life. She was always self-conscious about how she looked when she went out or felt that men weren't attracted to her. She was always comparing herself to other girls and became very depressed. She regretted allowing those women to get the best of her. She discovered later on that she was afraid to approach those men as a result of her own insecurities and comparing herself to other women. She then realized that she had lost out on many opportunities to establish relationships with men who had a real interest in her. A few of the guys she admired from afar, later in life approached her on several different occasion, sharing that they found her very attractive and wanted to talk to her, but she had always seemed so distant and closed off. Basically, she had no confidence in herself.

Mel took notice of the kinds of women some men choose. Some of these women were really skinny and some were bigger, not all had perfect, hourglass shapes. From these observations, she understood that these women attracted men because of how confident they were in themselves.

But they didn't use their body parts to get a good man. The ones who did think that having specific look or asset was the key to attracting a man seemed to attract the wrong kind of men. Women tend to compete with each other out of insecurities. Even beautiful women have some insecurity about themselves, and words affect them, too. Most women would say they can't stand to be around other women because they always compete for attention, whether it is from men or just for recognition. They need this to gain validation. Maybe they grew up without a father in the home, and a father will always let his daughter know how beautiful she is. A mother telling her daughter she is beautiful does not carry the same weight for a girl. She gains confidence in herself that way, because it is coming from a male perspective and she solidifies validation that she won't have to seek from outsiders.

Women who compete with other women for the spotlight (attention from men, etc.) often seem to be more insecure and end up alone, being used, sleeping with multiple men but never able to sustain a long-term, committed relationship. I notice these types of women always pretending that they have it all, but they have nothing to offer when it comes to an attractive personality. Insecurity is man repellent. No man wants to constantly feel like he has to keep reassuring his woman about how beautiful he thinks she is whenever another pretty or attractive woman pops up around them.

3

Remain Confident

There are two types of behavior that describe the different kinds of nature a woman can possess: passive and aggressive. The aggressive woman will try to insult and degrade another woman to build her self-esteem. But the reality is this: we come in all shades, races, shapes, and sizes for a reason. Be confident in yourself and comfortable in your own skin, knowing you are one of a kind. The passive woman is very subtle and low-key. She knows who she is and feels no intimidation about other women who are competing. She can relax, with the assurance that she can treat every other woman as she would want to be treated with no exceptions. She knows how to lift women up without feeling any level of insecurity or threat at any time. She knows one of the most important rules of womanhood: Never devalue yourself to compliment another person's issues.

There is no need to compare yourself to others or force someone (a man) to choose what you feel is a more desirable woman. There is a man out there for every woman. We come in many different flavors to choose from, and a man has freedom of choice just as you do. First and foremost, ladies, it is not your job to make a man love you, but it is your job to love yourself in such a way that a man cannot help but to love you. Women have a habit of comparing themselves to how we look and what men like. I've had my share of a lifetime of pain in dealing with some of these trifling sisters who felt they were the intelligent ones. Yes, women that fought and compete with me over a guy who may have an interest in me. I've had this problem since I can remember as early as my high school years. Situations like this only cause more tension and strife among women, because these women see themselves as better and more deserving of getting the guy than you are. When you consider these different kinds of attitudes, it shows how selfish some women can be because they are desperate to always be the center of attention because of one's self insufficiency, and their own insecurities. Maybe some of us women, act out of these different issues because of brokenness, bitterness, anger, promiscuity, deception, been cheated on, broken promises, fear, mistrust, and many other things, etc. These issues can lead to aggressive, self-defeating behaviors or acting out of lack of personal satisfaction. Physical fighting has been another way women contend over men; When things don't go according to their agenda, that's when they will wreak havoc on another woman's life.

Fighting for happiness, however, will always be a part of our human soul, because the struggle and warfare for love is real. Human emotions and the desire to be loved are part of the cosmos that we've been destined to experience in life. But until a woman can love herself, it will be hard for anyone else to truly love her. Women will put up with too much and will give their all, only to come out empty-handed. Sometimes multiple breakups can leave women traumatized. Because of that level of brokenness, going from man to man will leave a woman with all kinds of issues.

Ladies, even if you have not resolved these issues that we struggle with, they can cause us misery and unhappiness. We must find contentment within ourselves before the right man shows up, or we'll find a way to sabotage that, too, because it seems too good to be true. The reality of inner conflict is that you can't keep fighting to be with someone who isn't fighting to be with you. But on the other hand, it hurts when you have fallen in love with someone who played you like a fool, but it can be worse to choose to be a fool.

I remember when I was involved with this guy "Junior" who father my younger daughter by me. I was in my late twenties at that time, when he came whispering sweet nothings in my ear and I fell for the okey-dokey. I gather I was easily persuaded by his sweet words because he was a charmer so I fell deeply in love with him immediately. During the course of that time, I was devastated due to past abusive relationships with other men. So here I was, a young lady who had lived through cycles of abusive relationships from men who I had children with. They physically beat me, which left me emotionally scarred for years. I became like any other woman who was looking for love in all the wrong places. And along came a cute, light-skinned guy, Junior, was about five foot six—average height for a guy his age—and light in weight. He was not my ideal candidate for dating because he was from the Caribbean island of course. He appeared during a time when I was at my weakest point. Yes, I was so vulnerable that I wasn't looking for any relationship at all. But despite my silent years of heartbreaks, I managed to rebound and keep on living. He made me feel love and took my pain away. He knew all the right words to say and definitely knew to push all the right buttons. In other words, he swept me right off my feet. It wasn't too far into the relationship that he moved into my apartment and we were living together. A year or so into the relationship, I thought I was pregnant. I scheduled a visit to see my doctor and the results were confirmed positive. I could hardly wait until he got off from work to tell him the good news.

When he got home from work, I told him that I was pregnant, and he was as happy as I was. Nine months later, I gave birth to my third child seven-pound, fourteen-ounce girl. she is now 28 yrs old with three beautiful children. Also, there were two other children that I had from a past relationship with another gentleman which was a dead-beat dad. Lol. Yes, my first-born daughter is 34, and my second born 32, who are all up grown. Howbeit, that my children were small and in elementary school when I was dealing with "Junior. So my hands were pretty much full raising all three by myself.

Now I did mention how madly I was in love with the father of my last daughter? I thought the world only revolved around the two of us and nothing else mattered. I'm sure that some of you can identify with my story, how it feels to be so in love with the baby daddy. I was young and dumb, just beginning to touch the surface of things in my own life at that time. I built my whole world around him and refused to listen to what anyone else had to say about him. Herein, no one could tell me that both of us wouldn't be together forever, or at least that's what I thought. As far as I was concerned, I was building a life with him and raising our little family. Maybe I might have slipped into fantasy land. For the most part, I enjoyed spending family time together with him and my three children. Wherefore, I was so proud to be a mom for the third time, and I thought I deserved a more tangible relationship since I had given him a daughter. My idea of tangible was a marriage proposal, but I guess that was just my level of immature thinking kicking in. Little did I know, right? I already had two other children, Shameka and Ronell, from a previous relationship. I guess he said to himself "Why buy the milk when I can get the cow for free?"

After being with me for two years, he did not feel the need to commit to me for a lifetime. Within two years of getting into our relationship is when things began to shift and take a turn for the worse. During the first trimester of my pregnancy, I started receiving anonymous phone calls from a female. She called and threatened, me saying she would "kick my baby out of my stomach." The harassment continued until the woman finally revealed herself to me. She was the woman he had been seeing for nearly a year. He was cheating on me through the whole course of the relationship, and I realized it was time to say goodbye to him and his cheating habits because he wasn't going to stop. I then came to myself and said *this, too, shall pass*. It may have broken my spirit for that moment, but it made me the stronger woman that I am today.

Readers, you have to love yourself so you can give real love and accept real love. Every woman deserves to feel cherished, valued, and honored by her king.

4

Know Your Worth

Low self-esteem and its side effects are generally well known. However, low self-esteem can do major damages when a person has also been robbed of their self-worth. Lack of self-worth can make a person feel unworthy and make it difficult for them to love themselves as they should. Many dynamics are attached to low self-esteem, and it comes from many different aspects.

This issue doesn't only attack the physical parts of a person, but it affects them from the inside as well. For instance, a person with low self-esteem will view their outward appearance negatively, such as their lips are not puffy, their breasts are too small or too big, and their butt and hips are too wide or not wide enough. The list goes on and on. Low self-esteem affects the mind, body, and spirit in various ways. It truly takes life on a merry go round. One reason so many women go through plastic-surgery procedures to alter the supposedly unsatisfactory parts of their bodies is that they are unhappy with themselves. They don't like their physical appearances, their body shape, or different features of themselves. However, if how much can plastic surgery do for someone who doesn't like looking at the person they see in the mirror?

A self-esteem issue does not come from the outside of a person, it comes from within the person. They have to deal with the inward conflicts of their dilemmas, or nothing else will fix what is wrong. Some women become so desperate in their moment of pain that they try to cover up all their broken areas by replacing them with other things. It is not possible to find fulfillment until you learn to love the skin you are comfortable in. I won't say that every woman has low self-esteem, but some do. I speak so freely on this issue because I dealt with it through adulthood. I did not know how to love myself as a woman. I lacked the confidence to believe in myself, and that I could accomplish the dreams and goals I wanted to achieve. I had to motivate myself into getting things done because I never felt worthy of anything. I didn't feel like I was good enough to pursue the things in life I wanted. This is what low self-esteem can do to a person. One of my dreams was to get a degree, and I did it. In March 2015, I decided to enroll at Liberty University. I wanted to earn an associate degree in interdisciplinary studies. I graduated in 2017. Once I saw that I was able to achieve my dream and earn my degree, my entire life change completely.

Going back to school gave me a different perspective on myself. This was a life-changing moment that shifted my thinking. I was no longer carrying that low self-esteem around with me, not feeling unworthy or even the spirit of rejection anymore. For once in my life, I felt happy and my children were there to help celebrate my accomplishment. Another hurdle I had to conquer in life was learning how to drive. This was a big obstacle. I had a fear of driving and getting into car accidents. But I went to driving school to learn the techniques of driving. I learned all of the necessary maneuvers to finish the course. Then it was time to go for my license. Each time I took the driving test, I failed. I failed the test repeatedly until I became tired and discouraged. Because I had a problem with passing the driving test, I lost interest and left it behind. My low self-esteem returned because I was forty-nine years old and didn't have a driver's license. Hustling rides and standing at bus stops to commute was embarrassing for me. When I attended church services, I was ashamed to be seen standing at the bus stop while others drove fine cars.

But I never gave up. I went back to driving school for more lessons so I could be ready for the road test. This time, God blessed me with a Jewish instructor who was very helpful. He taught me enough until I was ready to go on the road once again. Finally, the day came and I walked into the driving test with the confidence that *I can do this*. I passed my road test with flying colors. I earned my license in May 2016. I was so happy and proud of how far I had come to achieve the things I wanted to complete.

I believe it was necessary to share my testimony of how I had to overcome low self-esteem in my personal life. I take delight in knowing that happiness is not just about being in a relationship with a man, but about finding fulfillment within.

Ladies, what about being your own happiness? How many times do we spend countless years trying to satisfy, please, and keep someone else happy more than we care about keeping ourselves satisfied, pleased, and happy? I would say that being happy for yourselves is a great sacrifice, but when you find it you find freedom. Knowing your self-worth makes a big difference. Then you will come to understand how valuable you are as a woman.

Here's A Nugget: The Value of a Gem

A gem is a very precious stone that is engraved and crafted into a piece of beauty. Therefore, ladies, you need to know that you are a gem to be admired and adored. When you know who you are, you walk with confidence and dignity. For instance, when a woman enters a beauty pageant, she knows she's up against many competitors. However, if she's a woman with a high level of self-esteem, then no other woman can intimidate her because she owns up to who she is. Know that you are a gem of class and beauty. Don't be afraid of feeling comfortable in your skin. This is a very important trait that all women should strive to possess.

5

Men Talk

Most men want a woman with enthusiasm for life and someone who will push and help him to reach his potential, a woman with a sense of humor. Men want a friend. The best explanation of my point that a man wants the woman he loves to be a friend came from a friend of mines named T.J. who is married to (Stace). The question was, "How has your marriage been able to last for so long as a couple?" His response, "I am in like with my wife." This man actually likes his wife. That word like to me is more powerful in a relationship than the word love. Why? There are many men who love their wife. Yet, they will spend the majority of their time with friends or at a strip club. Don't believe me? As a young college student, my brother's friend who owned a mortgage company hired me to work for him. During a slow day, he received a call that someone he knew was dying. Depressed by the news, he told me we were closing for the day. As we were driving home, I noticed he bypassed our normal exit, and I became concerned because I did not know this man that well.

When we stopped, I saw the side of a brick building with a nude woman painted on the front. It was a strip club. The woman—half naked—began dancing in front of him, and he quickly let them know he had no money. One stripper, who thought it was funny, came and sat down beside him. Long story short, he asked her what type of men went in there on a regular basis. She said, "Married men!" She went on to say, "I get paid to do exactly what I am doing right now, which is talking and listening." These men told this stripper that their wives don't listen to them.

T.J. liking his wife means that his wife probably pushes him to go out with his friends because he is so content to be around his wife. You want a man who will like you. Love is an action word. The man going to the strip clubs or going out with his friends every weekend is not showing actions of love. These are the actions of a man who is obligated to love due to his so-called commitment.

I recently came across one of my childhood friends Steven. He and I had an intense conversation on the subject matter "What Do Men like". We talked about the different approaches that men take when they are pursuing relationships as well. However, He shared with me about his great childhood friend who asked the question, "What do men really want?" Steven replied that he can give a list of things men need or desire from a woman, however, he would like to answer this question differently. He then said that when a man does not take the time to find his identity as a man, he will never be truly fulfilled in a relationship. When a man fails to address and face the issues from his past and his demons, a woman—a good woman—will not fulfill his soul. Steven was not sharing his thoughts based on what he thought he knew. He was sharing from the perspective of living it.

He then talked about a truly glaring indiscretion many men have experienced, the failure of parents and extended family members to teach them how to keep a good woman. More than fifteen years ago, he asked his childhood friends, men who have known him for at least fifteen years, "Did your family teach you how to keep a good woman?" All of them responded with the answer no.

He said he was taught, "Steven, don't get a girl pregnant and don't hit or disrespect them." That was it! I believe after hearing him share this experience with me, that this is what has made him be the better man than he is today: what family members instilled in him. I'm quite sure many men can testify or relate to Steven's experience in choosing wisely a good, quality woman who is willing to build a life with him.

6

Inner Conflicts

Steven also suffered from self-esteem issues, which began as a child due to his light skin and reddish-brown hair, for a long time. Thirty years ago, his low self-esteem stemmed from being seen and treated by his peers as someone different. One summer he grew from five foot five inches to five foot eleven inches, gained some weight, and start getting a new haircut called Jersey cut. Suddenly he was a popular guy during his junior year in high school. The girls who laughed and snickered at his appearance before began inviting him to different parties. As time went on, his man-hood issue turned to a subconscious level of anger and resentment toward women. When he recognized that his issues had affected his self-esteem, he grew tired enough to say to himself, *How dare you to make my life a living hell for two years, and now, because my appearance changed, I am supposed to acknowledge you?*

Let's now travel to his adulthood in professional circles. From years of not being accepted by women, he still carried himself in a way that showed he was waiting to hear someone laugh at his appearance. So, women who were interested in him began to question his sexuality because he did not respond to their advances. He had to deal with that.

Steven, a resident of South Carolina for the past ten years, has suffered from a lack of low self-esteem. .His professional experiences have included seven jobs, he was laid off four times, and suffered periods of unemployment that lasted as long as two years on one occasion. He was blocked from a better-paying job by a female African-American principal. He was laid off from a teaching job by an African-American male principal, even after his students scored at the high end of the end-of-year tests, which is how teachers are often judged. He experienced Spike Lee's old movie *School Daze*, wherein the south there are issues between light-skinned and dark-skinned people. Moreover, different men and women who get caught up in, and carried away with various completions in each other. This is quite typical but normal for both genders who find attraction towards one another. For instance, I was one that was attracted to light-skin brothers, because that was my preference. However, Steven genuinely was looking for the right women to stroke his manhood, and don't just focus on his skin tone. He wanted a woman to see the man that he is. Hey, at the end of the day a skin tone is just complexion but doesn't define who you are, nor is the center for happiness because of the color of someone's skin. But what matters how they treat you as a human being.

7

Relationships Matter

Relationships are an important part of our existence, for both men and women, who play a critical role in contributing to each other's lives. Because of our need for emotional care and wholeness, relationships cannot be excluded from the human equation. Honestly, it's the way we are made. That constant drive of needing to feel loved is a part of us that cannot be controlled. Because we yearn to be accepted by a man, we will stick to men who do not appreciate the woman we are, which can also lead to depression. At that point, they end up dominating our hearts, minds, and lives. Denial will lead women to desperate measures and other entities, such as suicide, self-hatred, promiscuity, murder, obsession, delusions, fantasies, and many other feelings or ways of acting out.

Even after all these changes, it leaves holes in our heart. Women were made to be loved and give love, just as men were made to be respected. Each woman wants to know that she can trust a man to protect her and provide a secure, supportive, and promising future. She needs that assurance to know that a man is strong enough to be consistent in his love toward her and faithful to never stray away from her. When a man does not confront himself and his issues, you as the woman can probably be the best thing next to the creation of indoor plumbing. Yes, he may not function well in a relationship. A flower cannot blossom without sunshine, and a man cannot live without love. You may say to yourself, *am I equipped to serve someone well in a relationship?* The answer is Yes. Men can hear us, give us respect, and pay close attention to what a woman is saying. It's an effort on the man's part and it's to our advantage because love is about putting someone else before yourself. Yes, we applaud men for their honesty royalty, dignity, and respect, because life is about making choices and taking chances.

My good friend Eric started his first program, Fathers with Voices, where he primarily works with separated and divorced fathers involved in custody and child-support cases. When these men contact his program, he can hear the brokenness over the phone. He can feel their rage, their depression, and their hopelessness. The greatest characteristic he says he has is his tone of voice. It is very light, calm, and at times without feeling. Why is this important?

He provided assistance for a father several years ago. Later, when contacted Eric him to provide an update on his case said the man told him, "Thank you for helping me… you didn't know this, but when I first contacted you and shared my experience with you, the whole time I had my hand on my gun." He later added that he was a cop. Let's just say, if Eric's tone was loud and indicating revenge, that situation could have turned out tragically.

8

Intimacy

Now celibacy is a gift from God and it is certainly celebrated when someone decides to abstain from any sexual contact. It's an effort by any man or woman to set boundaries and bring discipline to one's sexual lifestyle. I'm sure that many of us who struggle with abstinence know that it is not an easy task for anyone. But the hardship of maintaining our sexuality is real. Intimacy is just as important as the relationship, especially for women entering the dating life or marriage. Most women have no problem thinking dirty, because we have erotic thoughts. We can be naughty or nice; it all depends on the partner we're involved with and what our demands are.

It's really the chemistry in our genes that makes us act this way. It is perfectly normal. It's just part of our sexual nature. Whenever intimacy has occurred, we find it challenging to worry about what our partner thinks about our performance in the bedroom. So, you have to be as creative as possible to keep your partner a happy and satisfied camper. Since intimacy is precipitated, it is very important to us that men focus on whether his touch is gentle or rough, does it tingle or is it soothing, and how his skin and physique feel when we caress him. Woman love when men are great lovers. Now here is a factor about men: they will lie to get sex.

Yes, they will do whatever they have to do to get into the panties, from the manipulation of playing mind games to curiosity of seeing if she is easy to score with. These are women they won't commit to permanently, but just for the fun of it they just want a test drive to see how well she performs in bed. The game has not changed for as long as I can remember. It will only change when women wake up, smell the coffee, and realize they are not just for a man's pleasure, but are a valuable asset as their queen. Men like a challenge, but they don't like sex to be made complicated.

A highway has many exit and entrance ramps, plus other ways to gain access to it. Has your route ever called for you to drive on a highway with a heavy flow of traffic, so you tried to avoid it just so you can get to where you're going more quickly, but while driving on the alternate route, you lost your way while turning off at the wrong exit? In order to reroute your directions, you were looking for less traffic with easier access to get you to your final destination. Once you got back on the right route, you got to where you were heading. Finally, when you reach your destination, you gave a big sign and said, "That wasn't so hard after all." This is how men think when it comes to sex. They don't like when a woman makes it difficult for them to get access quickly. Women need to avoid men like this due to their promiscuous behavior, which can put a woman at risk. Intimacy can be met on so many different levels, it all depends on how serious an individual is or you have to opt-out of the game that's being played. Unfortunately, these are major danger zones that can lead to accidents.

9

Power and Sex

The church is a very, very important part of our spiritual lives. It is also a place of business to help improve our lives on a spiritual basis. I believe that the church was never intended to become a place for social entertainment, sex, and games. However, I've seen many ungodly behaviors and other things that transpired right before my eyes. The church us the number-one place where women come looking for love, marriage, and a mate. However, not everyone attends these spiritual assemblies for the same reason. There has been a lot of controversy around the church due to religious leaders who stand in the pulpit to preach the word, the women, who are Jezebels, and supposed the men of God who use power for personal gain. There has been a long history of pastors using their power in a destructive manner toward women in the church world. These issues within the church and its view toward pastors are: they, too, are worshipped, along with the God the pastors preach about. I imagine these leaders, too, have developed a god-like complex. This mentality amazes me, because how can one think that way when the very power they have been given was not given by themselves? Women are emotional human beings and some are smart enough to understand this fact about leaders taking advantage of the longing many women have for a fulfilling relationship. Some pastors are guilty of doing the same. Often you find that men in the faith have preyed on the weak and vulnerable women in the pews for pleasure, fun, and games. They know some women hunger to be validated by wealthy, influential men such as themselves who have the option of dating whomever they please. This is common among the many Afro-American churches. Women have a tendency to be attracted to power and fame. They find themselves caught up in the trappings of the limelight and success. This comes as no surprise, people wanting to be validated by applause and popularity in exchange for a glamorous lifestyle.

Have you heard of first-lady drama in the church? Yes, this happens to be the case. They all contend and compete against each other to be the leading first lady. Many women can be found fighting for the seat of honor, recognition, and power. They don't care who they have to hurt to obtain it, just as long as they get there.

I understand human error, but some men have all kinds of dilemmas such as pornography, sexual addiction, and sleeping with multiple partners. I believe this may be a major problem of controlling the fleshly part of their manhood. For others, their sex drive is completely out of control. These actions are common among religious leaders who are called to serve in many different capacities. There must be standards in place that would help counsel those women who are bruised, hurting, and looking to feel love. The woman feels a need. She goes to a pastor, seeking Christian guidance and counseling. Christian counseling and guidance can only be accomplished when the person is sharing the word of God and following it up with godly actions. When a woman goes to seek counsel from a pastor, and his moves toward a relationship to satisfy his own flesh, he has now entered into the carnal universe. We must be mindful, ladies, that pastors are not God. An anointed man of God understands his power comes from God and God is a spirit. He understands that God is not flesh, and he is holy. This means that the power given to this man of God is meant to be used in a holy manner. The moment that flesh enters in, God steps out and Satan has captured the mind of the pastor. A pastor's power does not exceed God's power. This means that before you go to your pastor, you should go to God first because he is unlimited in power and the ultimate power. Man is always at risk of falling. Do not put your total trust in a pastor, because the pastor still exists in a world where sin is prevalent. When a man is called to preach the gospel, he is not suddenly removed from humanity. If you are going to seek counsel from a pastor and you begin to develop feelings or you feel he is behaving in an ungodly manner, terminate the counseling sessions immediately.

10

Disturbing Behaviors

We live in a very diverse, multicultural society that has changed over the course of time in technology and medically. Out of all the different species here on the planet, scientists will tell you that human behavior is one of the most difficult concepts to comprehend. With all of the research and experimentation they do, they are still left baffled and nodding or even scratching their heads over the many brain activities that are associated with human behavior. Even in the medical fields doctors and psychiatrists are left perplexed, trying to fully grasp and understand all there is to know concerning the range of human behavior.

Whoever heard of the wide range mental illnesses running rampant among our nation? There are thousands of people who suffer from bipolar disorder, which is a chemical imbalance in the brain. This illness is real and can be treated if monitored by the right group of practitioners such as psychiatrists, therapists, and counselors who specialize in this type of care. This problem does exist and is common among women. Some may not even admit to their psychological dysfunction. Some people may not have a clue of knowing they are ill, and this may be a contributing factor to why they practice self-defeating behaviors. I'm speaking in terms of being incapable of committing to a long-term relationship. Others can't seem to stay true to one partner or have multiple sexual partners and are very unsettled. Wherefore, mental illness is common in our culture. There's a category for individuals such as these types of women can be seen, like fragile beings who do not have a backbone to stand on. They can be vindictive, dangerous, and brutal. You must watch out for dangerous-minded women who will do everything in their power for love, even at the cost of hurting a bystander. Have you ever seen a show called *Cheaters*? It comes on the air in the wee hours of Saturday mornings. Or perhaps the show *Snap* that discusses the matter of homicide cases with couples that murder in an act of rage because of jealous lovers. All this is done in the name of love. These have been commonly known as disturbing behaviors among women and men in today's society.

From reality shows television to those who are successful in the world of entertainment. Mental illness that has gone undiagnosed occurs around social events, political arenas, even in workplaces, and to the gathering in the household of faith. This problem has always existed in society. We can find much history about women's emotional dysfunctions in relationships from looking through pages of the Bible until the dispensation we live in now. It never ended the war of strife and confrontation from a woman's fighting for love or to win the heart of a man. The truth of the matter is this: we all want love in our lives because of our human emotional needs. You can find just about anywhere on planet earth women fighting over men. Or fighting to either have or take another woman's husband. You have women who are just plain evil and conniving with all kinds of ulterior motives for stealing a man from another woman. I call them men stealers, because they don't feel self-sufficient enough to get a man on their own. Some of them enjoy hurting another woman just to make themselves feel good. I consider women like these to be home-wreckers. If you would access their backgrounds, some have probably been hurt by a man they were in love with, and it affected them mentally. Maybe some women have never been able to pull themselves back together again, leaving them with all kinds of psychological dysfunction. I imagine that many times we don't go seek mental treatment or counseling for those unresolved issues. These kinds of psychological disadvantages can lead to other things, such as stalking, harassing, and obsession, which leads to even more disturbing behaviors.

Again, unaddressed issues can be the result of mental breakdowns. These are untapped areas where men should not play with our emotions. The movie *It's a Thin Line Between Love and Hate* addresses this issue, as the cause of why so many men feel regret for partners with whom they have a soul tie. Because they were so busy being fascinated by what they saw on the outside, they are sidetracked by beauty and booty but are unable to discern the intention of that woman. The man sees a woman, decked out from head to toe, wearing glamour-girl makeup, but that is only the outward appearance. He can't see all of the emotional baggage that women are carrying. Looks can be very deceiving. This is what causes men to get tricked, because they see the body but not the mind.

11

Christian Worldview

I believe that every human being has been given the gift of life to experience the value of love and relationships right here on earth. Every human being is uniquely created with the ability to comprehend and understand the visible, physical environment we dwell in. Our mind is one of the most powerful organs, and it ties us to our human emotions. It has a great influence on how we perceive things in the natural world as well as one's spiritual awareness. Human behavior does permit us to develop and grow through various thinking modes, even while we are in the stages of learning different ways in our lives. Our mind is constantly going through the process of discerning many challenges as we begin experimenting with relationships, family, love, intimacy, marriage, friendships, and so on. This comes via a wide spectrum of interaction with diverse cultures and customs on every level. As human beings, we have that right to express our likes and dislikes, who to date and marry, and many other things that we engage in. There is a wide range of Christian values and principles that are a part of our culture.

As we mature from childhood to adulthood, we are trying to find our identity by what and whom we associate with. Because of God's infinite wisdom and power, he never designed us all to think alike. We all have our own principles with regard to our beliefs and how they are to be applied to our everyday lives and our Christian values.

From a natural point of view, it's an honor and a privilege to have the freedom to choose and make our own decisions and choices in life. The infinite God has given us the options to navigate and explore life through our human nature. Our intellect and the human mind together are how we develop and think about many theories and behaviors that challenge our ability to grow, change, and develop with time. Upon viewing the church, I always thought of it as a place of tranquility and peace. For others, however, it can be seen as a war zone.

Some people think that everyone comes with the mindset to assemble themselves to receive the Teachings of Christ for their enrichment, so that we all may receive instructions and guidance for the soul from our spiritual leaders. But that's just not the case in every situation. There are all kinds of people who turn to religion with hidden agendas. Or they come looking to glean for their selfish greed. Whether it may be the first-lady positions or whatever, such an attitude can lead to, arrogance, cold hearted, and unlovable. Most of the time, a woman so desperate and eager for a first-lady position hungers for power and to be in control. However, some woman can't even control their own home and family lives, but want to be over the church.

As Christians, we must value the sanctity of our bodies and guard our spirits against the many impurities that can become a catastrophe to our relationship with the Lord. This is why it behooves us to carefully consider who we cohabitate with, because these decisions are considered soul ties that can cause long-time regrets and cannot be taken back.

12

The Denial State

Some woman goes through a stage of denial when the relationship doesn't work out. This is the most challenging and difficult moment that a few of us will have to face. I'm talking about when you're still in love with your partner who no longer wants you or the relationship. Now I must acknowledge that not every woman is mentally strong enough to handle breakups. Rather than accept that the relationship is over, some refuse to let go.

Have you ever experienced a breakup in a relationship that you weren't ready to have end? Or you did everything in your power to keep the relationship going because you still had feelings for your former partner? Some women will be driven to a state of delusion and denial by an unwanted breakup. Others may become oblivious to truth and block out what is reality. A woman can, in fact, delude herself into finding ways of using manipulation to keep hold of a man.

Manipulation is a very powerful tool, especially when used in a negative way. This is an old trick that women and men have used to control situations. Women use manipulation often to gain love and affection or even sex games for pleasure. When they feel they're losing their grip on a man they want to keep connected to them, they will manipulate any way they know how, through lies, schemes, traps, and deception. Delusional is the best way these emotions can be described when women are in pursuit of happiness. It's a process that many woman may have experienced in her lifetimes when she falls into a state of denial. She completely abandons what is reality and slips into that world called fantasy.

When your mental status has been affected psychologically following a breakup, it can be a mental strain that creates all kinds of delusions. Every woman may not have the capacity to handle being left by a man; she may have a mental breakdown to the point she becomes dysfunctional. In cases like this, some behavior may call for a physiological evaluation. Most will deny that there is anything wrong, but they would rather lie to themselves than accept that a relationship has ended.

When a man tells us he doesn't love us anymore, believe him. Most of the time men are telling you the truth. The game for love has been around for millennia. Love cannot be forced upon or manipulated against another person's will.

13

Table Talk

Table talk is what every woman should look for if she finds herself in the circles of love, but is still unhappy. Table talk is conversation to help you heal from a broken heart. Women who continue to get involved with men who are sore losers, men who have problems with being devoted to one woman, men who are liars, and those who continue to go from one woman to the next women because they're good at what they do. I know that some women can identify with me that there are men like this who keep playing emotional games with your head. Yes, they promise a ring, but never keep their word. Let the truth be told that issues like these can be damaging ad devastating for women.

These issues leave our hearts stained with mistrust, feeling abuse and used. I hate to see men take advantage of a woman sexually because she was weak and vulnerable. Does this sound like you? Yes, women who desperately want love at any cost and truly want to be committed to the man she loves right now. Some of these brothers know that this woman loves you, but you refuse to commit to her. Ladies, you cannot afford to keep spending your time on men like this, men who continue to give you nothing but heartaches and pains.

Real talk, girl, you have to want more for yourself then others want for you. If you see yourself in this continuing cycle, then it's time to stop wasting your life on these dead-end relationships. Get away from relationships that aren't taking you anywhere and do not add any value to your life. Let me say this: I'm not a therapist, but my advice to women is to stop wasting your precious time waiting on a man to marry you. Have you ever thought that maybe the man you so eagerly want to marry isn't worthy of loving you? Some men don't know how to love a woman properly, mainly because he doesn't how to love himself. Ladies, we have to think more precisely and clearly about what direction you are heading toward when building new relationships. These are the questions you should be asking yourself if you're planning to establish new a new relationship:

What do you expect in a new relationship?

Do you plan to set boundaries as to what you will or will not tolerate from men?

Make up your mind that you will work on self-improvement and develop yourself. See this as your season for change. However, be open to getting some therapy for inner healing to better prepare you for a healthier relationship. Most importantly, learn how to be happy with yourself before trying to make someone else happy. True authenticity for welcoming new romance is to first apply medicine to old wounds. You'll find freedom. Be ready for new doors of opportunity that will bring you the joy you long for. Say this with me: "I choose to be happy." And learn to love yourself. Remember, happiness begins inward and shows outward, for yourself and those around you.

14

Coffee Break

Sometimes we become uncertain of when we will meet the man of our dreams. In other words, when will we land the right opportunity to finally settle down with the right one? Sometimes in life you have to be patient until the time comes for you to settle down in a marriage. But sometimes women aren't ready for marriage because we have some unfinished business that needs to be fixed. Especially if you're women with a spirit of promiscuity that keeps you running from man to man and from bed to bed without considering your dysfunctions. Have you ever stopped to think that sleeping around with multiple partners is unhealthy and risky business at the same time?

What about other issues, when women find themselves afflicted with sexual addictions? Ladies, if you find yourself in one of these categories then maybe stepping away from dating for a while is what you need right now. Yes, that's when you need to take a coffee break, which is nothing more than stepping away for a minute or two, to rest continue what was started.

This is pretty much how I see things in life from a philosophical point of view. Sometimes life has a way of beating you down and can become overwhelming when you take on too much. However, when you find yourself getting frustrated and moody because things are not flowing the way you think they should, it's time to take a break. You need to step away from all of the things that create anxiety, worry, anger, and a trillion other things that make you miserable. Also, if you are in a meaningless relationship that keeps your life upside down, don't be afraid to step away. Maybe your life needs to be detoxed to clean out all of the clutter that is in there. If you are single, you might be tired of being alone and you want to be married. This is normal and quite typical for both genders to feel like this.

All of these issues are things that have to be addressed before considering marriage. You might ask why that is. The answer is that if you find it hard to be committed to one partner in a relationship, then you're not ready for a committed marriage. And if you do find the right man that you want to marry, then all of these problems that you haven't dealt with will spill over into your marriage.

Now, how many of us are ready for marriage when our spirit is broken and wounded from previous relationships? Yes, some of us have been badly scarred yet refuse to seek the help of a therapist to put us back together again. Ladies, if you feel that counseling would be of some use for unresolved relational issues, then why not go treatment. After all nothing beats a failure but a try. I think finding the right therapist makes a bit of a difference, because there is the comfort to opening up and share all of those men issues that you never dealt with. Also, counseling would be a steppingstone in shedding some light on why we keep falling for the wrong guys or why we keep being attracted to men who want us physically but are emotionally unavailable. This kind of behavior is toxic and unhealthy to keep indulging in. Maybe seeking counseling would be a turning point in helping many women break free from the trappings of unsuccessful relationships. If you have found yourself stuck in the trenches of an unsatisfying relationship, then you may want to hire a good therapist to help you resolve those problematic behaviors and feelings you've been dealing with.

I feel that therapy is like medicine that has to be taken to help someone get better. I gather that once a person gets the proper treatment that is needed, you should be able to recover enough not to go back down the wrong lane. With treatment and recovery, you can make better decisions for yourself and others around you. Moving forward and preparing for marriage is a big step to embark upon. Having the right man come into our lives when so many women are emotionally and mentally unprepared to give themselves to the next man is a true gift. If you haven't healed from past relationships you were in, then you are not ready to move forward to marriage. So pause, rewind, and push play while taking all the coffee breaks you need to recover.

15

The Opposite Side Of The Train

Psychology is a scientific study of thinking, actions, and behaviors from a pschological point of view. We're looking on the other side of the train to see that men have complex issues too. Men deal with the same crap women go through in relationships. They are looking to achieve happiness and have a successful partner who has something to offer and bring to the table as well. A man may not tell the women he's dating what conflicting issues he may have dealt with in previous relationships, either. However, women have intuition. We know how to read between the lines when a guy is holding back information.

Have you ever stepped into a subway station and the track goes two ways, for both trains to run the opposite direction. However, one side of the track says east and the other says west. The signs are visible to help you navigate where you're going. Sometimes there might be a delay in the daily operations of the train, which will cause them to run off schedule. But to keep things running smoothly, you might hear a voice over the loudspeaker telling you that there is some difficulty with the trains, so please be patient. And the train will be flagged to ensure that none of the trains are running too close behind each other on the track since this can cause a collision, and someone is bound to get hurt. I used the train scenario as a demonstration for men and relationships. So ladies, let's not be men bashers, but be understanding to the dilemmas that men go through. I believe that not every man is out to dog a woman out. However, there are some good, wholesome men out there, you just have to know where to find them.

Just as women are looking for love, so are men looking for love too. As men and women cross paths in everyday life, men speak the same language women speak, they just use a different tone. They're in search of a good woman who will hopefully love, care for, and treat them with respect. But what happens when the tables are turned and you see a woman dogging the man out? How do we feel about situations like this? And know this, some men do suffer from low self-esteem issues. That's why some men can't seem to keep their penis in their pants. But of course, they make excuses for their behaviors with speed. However, in in spite of their actions, men are human also and they deserve love, care, and respect, just as we do.

So, right now I am looking through another view of men and relationships from the opposite side of the train. I have a male friend named Richard, and Richard is a pretty decent gentleman and not bad looking at all, but his self-esteem is very poor. He does a lot of maintenance to keep himself looking well. Richard is a sharp dresser and wears a lot of expensive, name-brand clothing. Also, he keeps a very good job, making an excellent salary. Last time I heard that him and his woman have three children and they were living in the hood. But there are times when Richard is having relationship problems and he doesn't like sharing his business with anyone. At least from what I know, the relationship he and his baby mother are in is toxic. Now I have heard through the grapevine that his girlfriend Natalie is always out in the streets drinking, partying, and leaving him with the responsibility of their three kids. Word is around that she is an unfit mother. Richard shares with me on several occasions that she cheats on him with other men. I just can't imagine how he feels, knowing the mother of his three kids is sleeping with some other dude.

Somehow, when things get hectic and out of control, Richard will either call me or his homies to get our advice. I know that some men have dealt with the same or similar cases like Richard's. But here is the part that bothers me: When a dude is trying to love his women but the relationship is toxic and his baby mother treats him like a dirty dog. He works hard to keep food for his kids and buy them the clothing they need and contribute to some bills in the household. Richard continues to provide and give his children's mother the support she needs. Unfortunately, he is living in the street because the mother of his children keeps putting him out.

In an instance like this, I don't think any man should tolerate a woman mentally and emotionally abusing him in this way. I hope that Richard will find the inner strength to walk away from this dead and toxic relationship he's in.

Some men would rather stay in an unhealthy relationship just to be love. You have to realize that any person who treats you like the scum of the earth isn't worthy of your love. A relationship that takes you nowhere in life isn't worth of staying in. However, if you are constantly being belittled by your significant other, then you need to let it go. It is only a matter of time before your spirit is bankrupt and you find yourself with nothing. However, if someone keeps you feeling miserable then you need to get out of that dead-end relationship and run for your life. You have to find your peace until the right person who adds to your value and enjoys you comes along.

16

The Married Life

Marriage was instituted by God to bring two people together in holy matrimony. People don't always married for the right reasons, nor do they respect the sacredness of marriage. However, not everybody will be married. Marriage is of the most serious decisions you can make. The fact that two people stand before the minister to vow their love for each other is powerful.

People rush into marriage for different reasons. Some people hold the idea of establishing a marriage with the person they have children with. Or their biological clock is ticking and they're feeling insecure because of their age. Some want to be committed to one person for a lifetime. But not all marriages make it to the end. Sometimes people fall quickly out of love with their significant other. And in many cases, people have married prematurely and are unprepared to weather the storms that come with life. Marriage is not just some idea, it's a lifetime commitment. So, be cautious about rushing too quickly to be married. I wonder if couples pay very close attention to the vows that are exchanged between one another. Because the vow to love, cherish, and obedience comes with a price. As the old folks used to say, don't get in the pan if you can't take the heat.

Recently, my best friend Karen shared with me how she thought about marriage. We were sitting in the living room having some couch conversations. And we managed to get on the subject of her marriage. She started by telling me how she saw marriage, that she wanted love, commitment, and to be taken care of. But the one thing that she did clarify was how immature she was when she said "Yes" to the proposal. After she married her husband Carlton she regretted being married. She finally admitted that she didn't have a clue about what marriage meant.

The problem with my friend was she still wanted to hang out with us. Her other friends and I were into partying, drinking, and men before God saved me. When Karen's husband was away in the Army she hung out with us. And she was cheating on her husband with another man. We were a friend who didn't care about her marriage. We never stopped to think that Karen was a married woman, all we wanted was to do our thing. When her husband came home on the weekends, she pulled away from us to spend time with him. Nevertheless, none of her friends, including me, had respect or regard for her marriage.

I remember when Karen told me that her husband almost caught her with the other man. Okay, she claimed she and her boyfriend were hanging out at her sister's apartment. While they were there, she heard a knock on the door and she knew it was her husband. She quickly told the man she was messing around with to leave, because her hubby was knocking on the door.

I remember her sister's apartment because I use to hang out there all the time. The bedroom window had a gate with a key for emergency purposes. And there was a fire escape that led to the ground floor. Her boyfriend quickly climbed out of the window and ran. Finally, she rushed to open the door for her husband, and he asked where is that nigga. My friend was so nervous she told him there was nobody there. But she sighed with a relief that she didn't get caught. The marriage did end in divorce, though, because she later found out that her husband was cheating on her too.

So they both had issues with being faithful to each other. However, the one thing that my friend said she learned from her married lifestyle was to never make a big decision while being immature. I can identify with making a big decision to be married to someone until death.

When I married my husband Keith he was not the man of my dreams, or at least that's what I thought. When I married him, we were both of the faith, but that was a lie. After I left my worldly lifestyle of sin and pleasure, I had to stay clean before the Lord. So the right thing for me was to practice abstinence. I stayed single for many years before I said I do. But then the enemy set a trap for me to fall into and sidetrack me off my course. But the enemy knows just what women are like. So he sent me my husband and I thought it was a godsend. Later in our marriage, I found out that he wasn't sent from God, but from Satan. Things started going sour in our marriage within the first year. I discovered that he was on drugs and it waged war on my life. I tried to the best of my ability to hide his drug issues from my three children, but that didn't work. They all recognized that something was wrong with him. So my husband being on drugs put a strain on the marriage.

Suddenly, my entire household began crumbling to the ground. We all became like total strangers living under the same roof. I attempted to help my husband by attending drug-addiction recovery classes with him. I remember going with him one day to be a support system, but that didn't work. He didn't have enough strength to fight his demons. As the years passed, I saw no changes in his behavior. He continued getting high on those drugs and I became very depressed. I didn't know who I was anymore. We argued and fought like cats and dogs.

But I was determined to find a way out of this nightmare. There was a part of me that tried to fight to keep the marriage alive. I would be lying if I said I didn't. But there was the other, frail part of me that said to let it go. Sometimes you have to pay attention to the details in your life. In that life, all I remember is the darkness of his demons trying to take me out. However, I had to get up from that dark place and live because I had three children who needed me.

I finally made up my mind to walk away from the marriage. I had relocated to Maryland and continue raising my children. God had to heal me mentally, emotionally, and spiritually, from the inside. I was able to stand again and claim my freedom as a woman of worth. I then moved forward in filing for divorce, which ended the marriage. I needed to bring closure so I could be free to love again. Now I'm healed, delivered, and set free. I needed to go through that so I can help other women be healed.

Never settle and become comfortable in dysfunctional relationships or a marriage that is sucking the life out of you. Permit yourself to be free. You deserve someone who will love you as you love them.

17

Love and Happiness

Love and happiness are a blended combination that a woman expects in her relationship, with no exceptions. Even at the risk that love will hurt us, we still long for that feeling in every part of our being. When we analyze love, it's an action word that can be described as a strong emotion that all human beings need. It will only be manifested genuinely within our human efforts when it can be shown by a demonstration. It's an emotion that should never be compromised.

It is every woman's dream to find happiness and fulfillment in her relationships. Happiness is not an outward sign, as an emotional expression on one's physical appearance, but it comes from within. Oftentimes we use men as an alternative for happiness, which is our way of feeling complete or whole. But on certain terms, this is not always the case; happiness is an inner expression of laughter and smiles, an incredible emotion that is already there. So, when a man comes along, he should be the accessory that complements us, the gift wrap on the package.

Love goes deep and beyond all human capacity to fully comprehend it entirely. We know that it exists among us and was placed in our hearts to experience it in monogamous relationships. The power of love demands action to be demonstrated, more than just promising words. It is not defined by materialistic possessions given in exchange for sex or acceptance but is shown through acts of gratitude and affection. Love should never be compromised because it is so precious and valuable when you find your soul mate to share it with.

It is every woman's dream to find happiness and fulfillment, whether in a relationship or marriage in hope that she will obtain a promising future with her dream man. We laugh a little and we cry some because love is about experimenting and life is exploring. It is a human emotion that's part of our makeup that we either embrace or reject.

Now I must admit, though, that the heart was made to hurt because it's a major organ. All human beings need a heart for survival, yet by classification, it is the most sensitive organ we possess. This is why women continue to fight to be loved and accepted because looking to find the right person to share that special bond of love with is challenging. Although we may get moody or may get on men's nerves over time, just know that love is still strong. Understand that love is the chemistry that sends many mixtures of emotions and requires much time and patience with the right partner. Nowadays people just have sex to get a few moments of pleasure. But love is deeper than most people think. Our body does react to emotions. One reason why women settle at establishing wrong relationships with men is that they don't value themselves. Knowing yourself and who you are making a difference to who you allow in your space. I tell women that loving yourself is a very healthy attitude because this shows us how to give and receive love. This creates an environment for happiness that doesn't require someone else to fill the voids.

It has been said that men are supposed to lead, protect, and provide, not control, manipulate, or abuse. When you find your soul mate, if it's true love he won't mistreat you, disrespect you, or neglect to fulfill his duty to you because love conquers all things.

Realistically, I think we don't choose who we fall in love with, it just happens spontaneously sometimes and we have no control over it. There are specific elements to love in how it flows that affect our emotions, especially when it comes naturally and purely, not forced or against one's will.

When people walk out of your life—the people who God has removed and replaced, the people who rejected and abandoned you, the people who talked about you and ridiculed you, the people who lied to or about you and cursed you, the people who mentally and physically abused you, the people who plotted to kill you, the people who had false motives and impure intentions, the people who came with hidden agendas—appreciate the people who stayed around through all the things you've been through because they're the ones who are worthy to go where God is taking you. For God to develop you for what he has prepared you for, he has to hide if we must live life in honesty and truth, be open and transparent, which leads to trust. Trust leads to friendship. This is something worth taking into account; this is the basis of friendship and trust, not money and warm-heartedness, but it's an essential ingredient if we are to live happy lives. A woman would hope for a partner to build a dynasty with, raise a family, and just live long happy lives in the hope that the spark of love doesn't die.

Is that too much to ask for?